Volume 78 of the Yale Series of Younger Poets

Picture Bride

Cathy Song

Foreword by Richard Hugo

Yale University Press
New Haven and London

Published with assistance from the Mary Cady Tew Memorial Fund.

Designed by Sally Harris
and set in Bembo type by Eastern Graphics.
Printed in the United States of America by
The Alpine Press, Inc., Stoughton, Mass.

Library of Congress Cataloging in Publication Data

Song, Cathy, 1955–
  Picture bride.

  (Yale series of younger poets; 78)
  I. Title.
PS3569.O6539P5 1983   811'.54   82–48910
ISBN 0–300–02959–4
ISBN 0–300–02969–1 (pbk.)

1   2   3   4   5   6   7   8   9   10

For my Mother and Father

For Douglas

Contents

Foreword

The final line of Cathy Song's book, *Picture Bride*, reads "Someone very quiet once lived here." This poem, *The Seamstress*, is about someone Song knows, or has fictionalized (and knows), and now speaks for. Parts of the poem, including the final line, might be said to apply to Song herself, the poet who "lived here." In Cathy Song's quietude lies her strength. In her receptivity, passive as it seems, lies passion, a passion that is expressed in deceptive quiet and an even tone. She receives experiences vividly and without preset attitude. Her senses are lucky to have remained childlike and reception appears to be a complete act. It would not be complete, however, without the poems.

Each section of the book is named for a flower, and Song's poems are flowers—colorful, sensual and quiet—offered almost shyly as bouquets to those moments in life that seemed minor but in retrospect count the most.

Song finds artistic kinship with two visual artists: the modern American painter, Georgia O'Keeffe, and the nineteenth-century Japanese printmaker, Kitagawa Utamaro. In one poem she pays homage to Utamaro's work; in another she concentrates on a single print, the details of which she has absorbed with such affection that finally she does more than describe. She presents as decades ago Ezra Pound wisely advised poets to do.

While Song admires Utamaro and finds the women in his prints creatures that she can recreate, she identifies with O'Keeffe's work. *From the White Place* is dedicated to her, and a sequence of five poems, *Blue and White Lines after O'Keeffe*, is based on five of her floral paintings. Song's personal relationship with O'Keeffe's work is as deep as her admiration of Utamaro's work.

Through empathy Song speaks for other women in some poems (*The Youngest Daughter, Lost Sister, The Seamstress*). She recreates these women just as she recreated the woman in Utamaro's print. On the other hand, Song's relation to O'Keeffe's paintings is allied to those poems in which Song speaks for and creates herself (*Waialua, Blue Lantern, For My Brother, The White Porch*).

Taste and touch are strong elements in the poems, although it is our sight that is most often engaged. And at times the sensuous and the sensual are inseparable.

> But there is this slow arousal.
> The small buttons
> of my cotton blouse
> are pulling away from my body.
> I feel the strain of threads,
> the swollen magnolias
> heavy as a flock of birds
> in the tree. Already,
> the orange sponge cake
> is rising in the oven.
> I know you'll say it makes
> your mouth dry
> and I'll watch you
> drench your slice of it
> in canned peaches
> and lick the plate clean.
>
> *The White Porch*

With her quiet tone Song engages a wide variety of experiences from the ecstatic to the distasteful. She accommodates experiential extremes with a sensibility strengthened by patience that is centuries old, ancestral, tribal, a gift passed down.

In the poem *Stray Animals*, a young couple tries to "trick nature" as the poem puts it. They make love, but want no children. However, nature "slipped in"

like the small animal
who began appearing then;
we attracted her with the heat
of our blue fire.

Since they are poor and have "nothing to spare," the couple refuses "the stray cat" admittance. They keep the cat out as they tried to keep the child out of their lives. The cat is like the developing child:

. . . I imagined the slight pressure
of her body, persistent as guilt,
on the other side of the door.
At night, we tried to muffle
her human noises with thick cushions
but the sound, cradled
in the iced trees, moaned through.

The cat is killed by a "blind vehicle," and later they see "someone stoop to wrap / the stunned pieces in an old sheet." The unwanted child grows now in the mother, and the mother has faith that, though she and her husband tried to trick nature once, nature will not try to trick them in return. Her husband's "large, untrained hands"

. . . will come to trust
themselves enough to guide
our frightened child through water,
out from the darkness of a dream.

Nature, as always, remains huge and neutral. And all experience becomes natural: some stray animals rejected so others can survive, stray animals killed because vehicles are blind, things done by us for each other (someone even tends to the remains of the cat), and children brought home safely even though they were once unwanted. We are all stray animals. This poem, perhaps more than any other in this collection, demonstrates a deep conviction

held by Song: what you receive belongs to you and be-
comes what you are.

Song does not shrink from the hard realities of the
societal and familial traps set for women. In *Lost Sister*,
she pays tribute to one who rebelled against China's sys-
tematic repression of women by immigrating. Perhaps
Song pays special tribute to her lost sister because the
psychic price of her rebellion was great and the rebellion
failed. The rebel finds herself in the new land,

> But in another wilderness,
> the possibilities,
> the loneliness,
> can strangulate like jungle vines.

Being a stranger in a new culture can lead to the most
outrageous fear of things unknown: "A giant snake rattles
above, / spewing black clouds into your kitchen." And
the demands of change are too much.

> You find you need China:
> your one fragile identification,
> a jade link
> handcuffed to your wrist.

The would-be rebel loses all chance for individual identity.
Like her mother in China, she has "left no footprints."
Sad as that failure seems, in her effort to rebel she still
put an ocean between herself and that past and at least
created an "unremitting space" others can cross or fill.

The familial trap is also harshly realized. In *The Youngest
Daughter*, for some time a woman has been caring for her
sick mother. The woman sometimes suffers migraines and
the mother in turn cares for her. The situation is cheerless.

> The sky has been dark
> for many years.
> . . . .
> It seems it has always

> been like this: the two of us
> in this sunless room,
> the splashing of the bathwater.

The daughter must bathe the mother. Though things seem better than usual on this day, once we see through her eyes we find the situation hardly wholesome.

> She was in a good humor,
> making jokes about her great breasts,
> floating in the milky water
> like two walruses,
> flaccid and whiskered around the nipples.
> I scrubbed them with a sour taste
> in my mouth, thinking:
> six children and an old man
> have sucked from these brown nipples.

A recurring theme in *Picture Bride* is a sometimes hidden but relentless desire for escape. *The Youngest Daughter* shows that freedom is momentarily known in the sudden dramatics available to the visual imagination.

> She knows I am not to be trusted,
> even now planning my escape.
> As I toast to her health
> with the tea she has poured,
> a thousand cranes curtain the window,
> fly up in a sudden breeze.

This desire to escape takes a delightfully fanciful turn in the poem *Primary Colors* when babies escape their parents, "sailing by in their runaway carriages, / having yanked the wind / out from under their mothers."

If we accept Cathy Song's background as it comes through the poem *Leaving* and through bits and pieces of other poems, we may sense the origin of, and even the necessity for, her passive/receptive sensibility. She need not rave or struggle. She has learned the strength of quiet resolve. As a poet she has discovered how hard work and the long act of writing and rewriting pay off if one remains passionately committed.

Cathy Song's poems do more than simply return to us a world vividly received. The world is *her* world and she alone has the artistic license to illuminate it. Some of her poems show a psychic and social range that, if much wider, would require a larger form than modern poetry with its inherited limitations can provide. Possibly a large work of fiction will be hers to write in the years ahead. For now, she offers her luminous world with candor and generosity.

Richard Hugo

I   *Black Iris*

Picture Bride

She was a year younger
than I,
twenty-three when she left Korea.
Did she simply close
the door of her father's house
and walk away. And
was it a long way
through the tailor shops of Pusan
to the wharf where the boat
waited to take her to an island
whose name she had
only recently learned,
on whose shore
a man waited,
turning her photograph
to the light when the lanterns
in the camp outside
Waialua Sugar Mill were lit
and the inside of his room
grew luminous
from the wings of moths
migrating out of the cane stalks?
What things did my grandmother
take with her? And when
she arrived to look
into the face of the stranger
who was her husband,
thirteen years older than she,

did she politely untie
the silk bow of her jacket,
her tent-shaped dress
filling with the dry wind
that blew from the surrounding fields
where the men were burning the cane?

The Youngest Daughter

The sky has been dark
for many years.
My skin has become as damp
and pale as rice paper
and feels the way
mother's used to before the drying sun
parched it out there in the fields.

Lately, when I touch my eyelids,
my hands react as if
I had just touched something
hot enough to burn.
My skin, aspirin colored,
tingles with migraine. Mother
has been massaging the left side of my face
especially in the evenings
when the pain flares up.

This morning
her breathing was graveled,
her voice gruff with affection
when I wheeled her into the bath.
She was in a good humor,
making jokes about her great breasts,
floating in the milky water
like two walruses,
flaccid and whiskered around the nipples.
I scrubbed them with a sour taste
in my mouth, thinking:
six children and an old man
have sucked from these brown nipples.

I was almost tender
when I came to the blue bruises
that freckle her body,
places where she has been injecting insulin
for thirty years. I soaped her slowly,
she sighed deeply, her eyes closed.
It seems it has always
been like this: the two of us
in this sunless room,
the splashing of the bathwater.

In the afternoons
when she has rested,
she prepares our ritual of tea and rice,
garnished with a shred of gingered fish,
a slice of pickled turnip,
a token for my white body.
We eat in the familiar silence.
She knows I am not to be trusted,
even now planning my escape.
As I toast to her health
with the tea she has poured,
a thousand cranes curtain the window,
fly up in a sudden breeze.

Easter: Wahiawa, 1959

1

The rain stopped for one afternoon.
Father brought out
his movie camera and for a few hours
we were all together
under a thin film
that separated the rain showers
from that part of the earth
like a hammock
held loosely by clothespins.

Grandmother took the opportunity
to hang the laundry
and Mother and my aunts
filed out of the house
in pedal pushers and poodle cuts,
carrying the blue washed eggs.

Grandfather kept the children
penned in on the porch,
clucking at us in his broken English
whenever we tried to peek
around him. There were bread crumbs
stuck to his blue gray whiskers.

I looked from him to the sky,·
a membrane of egg whites
straining under the weight
of the storm that threatened
to break.

We burst loose from Grandfather
when the mothers returned
from planting the eggs
around the soggy yard.
He followed us,
walking with stiff but sturdy legs.
We dashed and disappeared
into bushes,
searching for the treasures;
the hard-boiled eggs
which Grandmother had been simmering
in vinegar and blue color all morning.

2

When Grandfather was a young boy
in Korea,
it was a long walk
to the riverbank,
where, if he were lucky,
a quail egg or two
would gleam from the mud
like gigantic pearls.
He could never eat enough
of them.

It was another long walk
through the sugarcane fields
of Hawaii,
where he worked for eighteen years,
cutting the sweet stalks
with a machete. His right arm
grew disproportionately large
to the rest of his body.
He could hold three
grandchildren in that arm.

I want to think
that each stalk that fell
brought him closer
to a clearing,
to that palpable field
where from the porch
to the gardenia hedge
that day he was enclosed
by his grandchildren,
scrambling around him,
for whom he could at last buy
cratefuls of oranges,
basketfuls of sky blue eggs.

I found three that afternoon.
By evening, it was raining hard.
Grandfather and I skipped supper.
Instead, we sat on the porch
and I ate what he peeled
and cleaned for me.
The scattering of the delicate
marine-colored shells across his lap
was something like what the ocean gives
the beach after a rain.

Waialua

You lived near the sugarcane fields
on the north side of the island
where the sound of the ocean
could be heard through the ironwoods.

It was a long bus ride
I took on Saturdays; another hour
of waiting for you in the squinting sun.
When you didn't come,
I knew your truck was broken
and I would walk from the depot,
cutting through back fields,
crossing bones
scattered in the red dirt ditch.

The house was once a laborer's shack,
converted by you into a pottery,
reinforced by stilts
to keep out the water rats.
As I approached, scraps of smoke
flying above your roof
like flags in the humid air
were good signs. Pots were baking,
others dried on long planks of wood.
Their egg- and bean-shaped contours
flowered into pods and gourds,
exotic among the lank stalks of cane.
Creaking in the breeze,
the wood rose vine sometimes moaned,

arthritically, raining down seeds
and pelting the silt soiled clay,
mixing into the peculiar musky odor
I wore beneath my dress.

Inside, the walls were dark
like the walls of sleep. My eyes
blinked, adjusting to the shadows,
the shape of leaves
you grew everywhere.
My bare feet padded lightly upon
the itch of woven mats,
on their way to your room.
In your curved arms
my belly was a smooth bowl
you shaped, fleshed out and brightly
glazed. When the afternoons fell,
the night stalks sweetened,
breathing against the screen window,
meshing into barbed wire.

Blue Lantern

The blue lantern light
was like a full moon
swelling above the hush
of the mock orange shrubs
that separated our houses.

It was light
from your grandfather's room.

I remember the music
at night.
I dreamed the music
came in squares,
like birthday chocolate,
through the window
on a blue plate.

From his shakuhachi,
shavings of notes,
floated, and fell;
melted where the stillness
inserted itself back into night.
It was quiet then until dawn,
broken once by a single wailing:
the sound of an animal
whose hind leg is caught in a trap.

It was your grandfather
mourning his dead wife.
He played for her each night;
her absence,

the shape of his grief
funneled through the bamboo flute.
A ritual of remembrance,
keeping her memory alive
with his old breath.
He played unknowingly
to the child next door
who lay stricken by the music
transposed to her body,
waiting for the cry
that always surprised her;
like a glimpse of shadow
darting through the room
before she would drift off into sleep.

I knew you were in the room
just beyond the music.

This was something we shared.
Listening, my eyes closed
as though I were under water
in the blueness of my room;
I felt buoyant and protected.

I imagined you, his grandson,
listening and lying
in your small bed;
your head making a slight
dent in the pillow.

It was as though the weight
of his grief washed over
the two of us
each night like a tide,
leaving our bodies beached
but unbruised,
white and firm like shells.

Leaving

Wahiawa is still
a red dirt town
where the sticky smell
of pineapples
being lopped off
in the low-lying fields
rises to mix
with the minty leaves
of eucalyptus
in the bordering gulch.

We lived there
near the edge
where the orchids grew huge
as lanterns overnight
and the passion fruits rotted
on the vines
before they could be picked.

We grew there
in the steady rain
that fell like a gray curtain
through which my mother peered:
patches of depression.
She kept the children under cover.
We built houses within houses,
stripping our parents' bed
of pillows and sheets,
erecting walls out of
The National Geographic
which my father had subscribed to

for years. We feasted
on those pictures of the world,
while the mud oozed
past the windows
knocking over the drab green leaves
of palm fronds
as we ate our spinach.
The mildew grew in rings
around the sink
where centipedes came
swimming up the pipes
on multiple feet
and the mold grew
around our small fingers
making everything slippery
to touch.
We were squeamish and pale.

I remember one night
my sister screamed.
All the lights blinked on
in the house.
In the sudden brightness,
we rushed to her room
and found her crumpled
in the far corner of the bed,
her nightgown twisted in a strange shape;
her eyes were as huge as mine,
staring into the eyes of the bat
that clung to the screen.
Its rodent fingers
finally letting go
as my father jabbed its furry body
with the end of a broom.

For My Brother

You were born
in the year of the fish,
during the rainy month
when the pond brims over
and the trees in the gulch
grow leaves like spinach
and mold thickens
under the skin.

I was two
when from the broken water,
you came swimming,
slippery and smooth,
barely bigger than a tadpole.
You jumped
into father's surprised hands.
Mother wrestled to keep
your jellied body
cradled in her arm.

What a thirsty baby,
wanting seawater instead of milk,
you flipped happily in the crib
after your mushroom mouth
went slack, satisfied.

Peering into the cage of your crib,
I clung to the bars
while you slept,
the soft bones of your head

pared streamline in shape
as though in your dream
you swam through the air.

I watched your eyes gradually
slope back toward your ears,
your cheeks curved like slender islands.
How I envied that profile:
Egyptian and remote
like a delicate water-bearer of the Nile.

I carried you
through the mud to the stream
where crayfish were lobsters,
palm fronds umbrellas,
and watched you maneuver
in the stream,
pouring silver tongue to surface,
then diving once again
to navigate without words.

We each have become our own animals.
I am like the sheep,
woolly and silent.
I plant my belly on the hillside,
count myself to sleep.
I sit in the sun,
patient as a boulder,
like any proper sister.
And I know that I move differently,
using the alphabet
to spring from me an ocean,
to propel me through night waters.
This is my way
of swimming with you.

Birthmarks

Our child was conceived
in the desert.
During the summer solstice,
we walked through the dead orchard,
searching for the stream that ran through it
and the boy who ate apples
in the thin shade of the trees.
Both of us quiet, intent upon finding him.
The cottonwoods were shedding their fluff.
The air was clogged with white
drifting like feathers, like moths.

At Christmas we return to the room
where the blue light
lengthened that summer toward midnight.
The fireplace cold as an empty bowl.
The bedsheets stiff like the wind.

What begins as a tentative gesture
to speak of the child you once were,
roaming these hills, begins again
in the body of another. A boy's longing
for the unconcern of animals
and their docile, grateful sleep
beneath the stars.
Such longings remain with you forever
like the feeling of light that ripe June.
The world was stained with light.

The child of that summer
will be born to a man and a woman
who walked through old apple trees.
He will not have to be told this.
The imprint is there like a birthmark:
the brush of a moth
descending upon the curve of his ear.

II   Sunflower

The White Porch

I wrap the blue towel
after washing,
around the damp
weight of hair, bulky
as a sleeping cat,
and sit out on the porch.
Still dripping water,
it'll be dry by supper,
by the time the dust
settles off your shoes,
though it's only five
past noon. Think
of the luxury: how to use
the afternoon like the stretch
of lawn spread before me.
There's the laundry,
sun-warm clothes at twilight,
and the mountain of beans
in my lap. Each one,
I'll break and snap
thoughtfully in half.

But there is this slow arousal.
The small buttons
of my cotton blouse
are pulling away from my body.
I feel the strain of threads,
the swollen magnolias
heavy as a flock of birds
in the tree. Already,
the orange sponge cake
is rising in the oven.

I know you'll say it makes
your mouth dry
and I'll watch you
drench your slice of it
in canned peaches
and lick the plate clean.

So much hair, my mother
used to say, grabbing
the thick braided rope
in her hands while we washed
the breakfast dishes, discussing
dresses and pastries.
My mind often elsewhere
as we did the morning chores together.
Sometimes, a few strands
would catch in her gold ring.
I worked hard then,
anticipating the hour
when I would let the rope down
at night, strips of sheets,
knotted and tied,
while she slept in tight blankets.
My hair, freshly washed
like a measure of wealth,
like a bridal veil.
Crouching in the grass,
you would wait for the signal,
for the movement of curtains
before releasing yourself
from the shadow of moths.
Cloth, hair and hands,
smuggling you in.

Seed

We speak of naming our daughters,
still
inside you. Still inside me.
Separate, moist, quiescent.
Our meetings are conspiracies.
I bring the water,
you prepare the hunger.
I portion out the spirits,
the ritual of breaking bread.
You part the water,
come flying back to me
on boneless wings,
quiet fish.

Stray Animals

We thought we could trick nature
but she slipped in through the back porch
sometime after Valentine's Day
like the small animal
who began appearing then;
we attracted her with the heat
of our blue fire.
It was the candle in the window.

Seeking shelter, the stray cat
rubbed her orange fur against our door.
We never let her in,
having nothing to spare,
but I imagined the slight pressure
of her body, persistent as guilt,
on the other side of the door.
At night, we tried to muffle
her human noises with thick cushions
but the sound, cradled
in the iced trees, moaned through.
As the trees thawed, silence
returned in the shape of flowers.

One evening in early spring
we were drawn to the porch
because the moon was framed
in branches like a giant magnolia.
You brought out the telescope
and we took turns squinting
at the moon. It seemed to burn
off the color in our eyes.

That same night, the curry-colored cat,
pausing in a petal of moonlight,
was struck by a blind vehicle.
Later, sometime after midnight,
when we were throwing out the trash,
we saw someone stoop to wrap
the stunned pieces in an old sheet.

This morning, I feel
the pressure of that mute fur
in the weight of blossoms
now invading the trees.
Beneath the blue flowered flannel,
an invisible tension
continues to change the shape of my body.
You, too, are undergoing a transformation
as your large, untrained hands
will one day soon surprise you.
They will come to trust
themselves enough to guide
our frightened child through water,
out from the darkness of a dream.

Primary Colors

They come out in warm weather
like termites
crawling out of the woodwork.
The young mothers chauffeuring
these bright bundles in toy carriages.
Bundles shaped like pumpkin seeds.

All last winter,
the world was grown up,
gray figures hurrying along
as lean as umbrellas;
empty of infants,
though I heard them at night
whimpering through a succession
of rooms and walls;
felt the tired, awakened hand
grope out from the dark
to clamp over the cries.

For a while, even the animals vanished,
the cats stayed close to the kitchens.
Their pincushion paws left padded tracks
around the perimeters of houses
locked in heat.
Yet, there were hints of children
hiding somewhere,
threatening to break loose.
Displaced tricycles and pubescent dolls
with flaxen hair and limbs askew
were abandoned dangerously on sidewalks.

The difficult walk of pregnant mothers.
Basketfuls of plastic eggs
nestled in cellophane grass
appeared one day at the grocer's
above the lettuce and the carrot bins.

When the first crocuses
pushed their purple tongues
through the skin of the earth,
it was the striking of a match.
The grass lit up, quickly,
spreading the fire.
The flowers yelled out
yellow, red, and green.
All the clanging colors of crayolas
lined like candles in a box.
Then the babies stormed the streets,
sailing by in their runaway carriages,
having yanked the wind
out from under their mothers.
Diapers drooped on laundry lines.
The petals of their tiny lungs
burgeoning with reinvented air.

Hoolehua

for Kathy

He will rise with you one morning
when you will be wanting
to slow the motions down,
but everything happens so quickly now—
once the light lifts the dogs in the yard
from their sleep
and the hens begin to peck between
the boards of the house
and before one daughter is through,
your milk curdles with another
whose bright eyes will hurt you.
She is the one who brings you
cups of water
on trays with flowers.
Your father never moves
from his place where the porch slopes,
his bad eyes yellowing like the old sun
that washes the house each afternoon,
pulling from you
what the kiawe trees
have been burning off for years,
the slow fires.
The bones and the branches
gathered by the dogs
burn in your need to sleep.

Tribe

for Andrea

I was born
on your fourth birthday,
song of the morning dove
spilling from the guava tree.

Grandparents came to look at me,
the number-two girl
with dumpling cheeks and tofu skin.
They pinched and cuddled,
affectionately gruff, blowing garlic breath
across my unflinching face.
Lifting me into their brown speckled arms,
you stood guard, proud and protective
of this new fat sister, stern
like a little Buddha.

I rolled and rebounded,
gravity nestling its fist
in the center of my stubborn belly,
whereas you were lithe
with the speed of a rabbit,
quick and cunning.
You hopped to errands,
fetching this and that.

We shared papaya boats
Mother emptied of tiny black seeds
that resembled caviar
and eggshells Father hollowed for whistles.
Our lungs expanded
as though they were balloonfish

fluttering out noiseless tunes.
We blew our songs to the gulch
that brought the eucalyptus smell of rain.

I don't remember
going into the forest,
although you must have taken me
where the lilikoi vines
dripped sticky sap passionately,
their blossoms curling like bells or tongues.
I heard my first story from you.

Waving good-bye
at the edge of the grass,
you disappeared like a huntress
into the bushes, the only girl
in a gang of boys.
I knew bravery then
and what it meant to belong to a tribe
when you returned triumphant,
just as the afternoon showers broke,
with all their marbles
bulging in the pockets
of your leopard-spotted pedal pushers.
I heard your slippers slapping the mud
and, running to meet you
at the screen door,
I saw you laugh, tossing up something
sunlit and flashing into the air:
you told me how Arnold had cried
to lose his precious tiger's-eye.

Father and Daughter

You are holding my sister in your arms.
She is but a few months old.
It is your day off,
beginning the night before
when you crawled out from under
the hull of an airplane
and wiping the grease from your hands,
said good-night to the two black boys
holding the kerosene lamp,
the only light for miles around.

In the colorless photograph,
thirty years later,
I can almost imagine that sun
as you pose in the backyard:
the hot white light of Coral Gables
momentarily blinding the two of you
in a halo of light. The white
edges of your cotton undershirt
hazy as if on fire. My sister
in her baby dress, starched and sweet-smelling.

I would be born four years
later, an unexpected birthday gift.
My arrival snuffing out her pink candles.
But until then,
it would be the two of you
together with my mother waving
occasionally through. At the screen door,
her heart-shaped face smiling distractedly
as she wipes her hands on a kitchen towel.

The small child you carried
in your arms filled your breathing
with the clover in the world:
a clean and fragrant handkerchief
folded to your breast,
worth more than money in your pocket.
And the next day you could slide
back under the whale-shaped,
metal belly of the plane,
a flashlight propped in your mouth
like a Havana cigar,
because you had been given something:
a daughter to sing to you,
a small voice
emerging from the unlit room at dusk.

III   *Orchids*

Beauty and Sadness

for Kitagawa Utamaro

He drew hundreds of women
in studies unfolding
like flowers from a fan.
Teahouse waitresses, actresses,
geishas, courtesans and maids.
They arranged themselves
before this quick, nimble man
whose invisible presence
one feels in these prints
is as delicate
as the skinlike paper
he used to transfer
and retain their fleeting loveliness.

Crouching like cats,
they purred amid the layers of kimono
swirling around them
as though they were bathing
in a mountain pool with irises
growing in the silken sunlit water.
Or poised like porcelain vases,
slender, erect and tall; their heavy
brocaded hair was piled high
with sandalwood combs and blossom sprigs
poking out like antennae.
They resembled beautiful iridescent insects,
creatures from a floating world.

Utamaro absorbed these women of Edo
in their moments of melancholy
as well as of beauty.
He captured the wisp of shadows,
the half-draped body
emerging from a bath; whatever
skin was exposed
was powdered white as snow.
A private space disclosed.
Portraying another girl
catching a glimpse of her own vulnerable
face in the mirror, he transposed
the trembling plum lips
like a drop of blood
soaking up the white expanse of paper.

At times, indifferent to his inconsolable
eye, the women drifted
through the soft gray feathered light,
maintaining stillness, the moments in between.
Like the dusty ash-winged moths
that cling to the screens in summer
and that the Japanese venerate
as ancestors reincarnated;
Utamaro graced these women with immortality
in the thousand sheaves of prints
fluttering into the reverent hands of keepers:
the dwarfed and bespectacled painter
holding up to a square of sunlight
what he had carried home beneath his coat
one afternoon in winter.

Girl Powdering Her Neck

from a ukiyo-e print by Utamaro

The light is the inside
sheen of an oyster shell,
sponged with talc and vapor,
moisture from a bath.

A pair of slippers
are placed outside
the rice-paper doors.
She kneels at a low table
in the room,
her legs folded beneath her
as she sits on a buckwheat pillow.

Her hair is black
with hints of red,
the color of seaweed
spread over rocks.

Morning begins the ritual
wheel of the body,
the application of translucent skins.
She practices pleasure:
the pressure of three fingertips
applying powder.
Fingerprints of pollen
some other hand will trace.

The peach-dyed kimono
patterned with maple leaves
drifting across the silk,
falls from right to left
in a diagonal, revealing

the nape of her neck
and the curve of a shoulder
like the slope of a hill
set deep in snow in a country
of huge white solemn birds.
Her face appears in the mirror,
a reflection in a winter pond,
rising to meet itself.

She dips a corner of her sleeve
like a brush into water
to wipe the mirror;
she is about to paint herself.
The eyes narrow
in a moment of self-scrutiny.
The mouth parts
as if desiring to disturb
the placid plum face;
break the symmetry of silence.
But the berry-stained lips,
stenciled into the mask of beauty,
do not speak.

Two chrysanthemums
touch in the middle of the lake
and drift apart.

Ikebana

To prepare the body,
aim for the translucent perfection
you find in the sliced shavings
of a pickled turnip.
In order for this to happen,
you must avoid the sun,
protect the face
under a paper parasol
until it is bruised white
like the skin of lilies.
Use white soap
from a blue porcelain
dish for this.

Restrict yourself.
Eat the whites of things:
tender bamboo shoots,
the veins of the young iris,
the clouded eye of a fish.

Then wrap the body,
as if it were a perfumed gift,
in pieces of silk
held together with invisible threads
like a kite, weighing no more
than a handful of crushed chrysanthemums.
Light enough to float in the wind.
You want the effect
of koi moving through water.

When the light leaves
the room, twist lilacs
into the lacquered hair
piled high like a complicated shrine.
There should be tiny bells
inserted somewhere
in the web of hair
to imitate crickets
singing in a hidden grove.

Reveal the nape of the neck,
your beauty spot.
Hold the arrangement.
If your spine slacks
and you feel faint,
remember the hand-picked flower
set in the front alcove,
which, just this morning,
you so skillfully wired into place.
How poised it is!
Petal and leaf
curving like a fan,
the stem snipped and wedged
into the metal base—
to appear like a spontaneous accident.

Blue and White Lines after O'Keeffe

1. Black Iris
New York

I climb the stairs
in this skull hotel.
Voices beat at the walls,
railings
fan out like fish bones.

The doorman bends the darkness,
his eyes prying under the latch,
admitting nothing
but an infantry of roaches,
lapping up the turpentine.

Old woman,
mouth stuffed with socks,
waits outside the door.
Her son, catwalking along the sill,
chips away at the enamel on my sink.
He thinks it is hard candy.

His girl friend is the opera singer
who lives inside my pipes.
The radiator hisses in the corner,
drawing warm blood,
deflating my tomatoes.

And I, the young painter,
once again,
prepare to dine alone.

I stare into the palette,
imagine green in my diet.
Peeling back the tins of sardines,
these silver tubes of paint,
lined like slender bullets:
my ammunition.

2. Sunflower for Maggie
Taos, New Mexico

Because you preferred Van Gogh's
mutilations:
that scrawny reproduction
tacked under the kitchen clock,
with its frayed edges
curling like the corn skins
we shed all summer long.

I wanted you to remember
the date on the calendar,
your birthday,
the way you were smiling in the garden.

3. An Orchid
Makena Beach, Maui

I wear hats now,
like halos,
as I haul my easel into the shade.

Since the first light,
the men have been gone.
I cross myself
with ti leaves:
a gesture they do not understand.

Strung along the beach
like cowrie shells,
the island children
squat and brood for hours.
Their eyes are the eyes of old fishermen.

Under the ironwoods,
Filipino women chatter,
shredding coconuts for the noon fire.
Their bird language
rises with the smoke
that spirals up in the blue air:
arms braceleted with tortoiseshell,
beckoning me to join them.

But here, in my safe shading,
I have all the colors I need
and already, too many clothes.
What tropical plants
I cannot eat,
I can use for dyes.
On my side of the beach,
I comb the tide pools for algae,
pound the blue organs of jellyfish
into pulps for sea green pastels.
These islands
have swollen my appetite;
still, each fish, fruit and flower
diminishes me.

If the bright sun
could only be kinder,
I would crawl out of my sensible shoes
and wear the humid stillness

like the young wahine
running to meet the first canoes.
They bear the sweet-sour
odor of mangoes
that rises from welcoming limbs.

4. Red Poppy

    In Andalusia,
it is the men
who are afraid of the darkness,
charging into the night like bulls—

        dry grain leaping into the wind,
        riverbed coughing up stones
                until Gibraltar)

to meet another darkness.
Their fathers instruct them,
holding the blade;
while the women sleep,

        the back-bent hills
        hold olive fields.

5. The White Trumpet Flower
   Sun Prairie, Wisconsin

"Women are like flowers,"
you said, for years
I despised myself
and you—
Mother
and Aunt Winnie in the garden,
arranged like lawn chairs,

smiling full of babies and detergent.
The hems of your white dresses,
sprigged with cloves and lavender,
fenced my playground. You were happy then,
happiest when I played
with the doll family.
They bored me;
I disliked their fragile bodies
and waxy yellow hair
and none of them looked like my father.
But I played with them,
tossing their useless bodies up into the air,
because you were pleased and smiling.
But soon, smiles were not enough.
I discovered my own autonomy then,
crawling out from your wide skirts
and into your flowerbeds,
where I proceeded to crucify the dolls,
decapitating your crocuses.
You scowled (and I clapped),
saying, "Georgia,
you are like the dogwood . . .
a homely name for a goofy flower.
There's just no potential. . . ."

Dear Mother,
you would not like it out here;
in Abiquiu there are no flowers,
not your kind of weather.
I have lived without mirrors and without men
for a long time now—
but I can feel my own skin,
how it is parched and crinkled like a lizard's.
And if you looked at my eyes,
you would exclaim, clicking your tongue,
"Crow's feet! So young!"
But I like to think of them

as bird tracks, calligraphy in the sand.
Still, you would appear as constricted
as a porcelain flower vase;
claustrophobic in its own skin,
in mild-mannered sitting rooms.
Shrinking,
when something wild
like a dog or a young child
comes running and panting through,
upsetting its mantelpiece equilibrium.
Yet, I am here, Mother.
I have come to rest at your feet,
to be near the familiar scent of talc,
the ticking of the china clock,
another heartbeat.
It has taken me all these years
to realize that this is what I must do
to recognize my life.
When I stretch a canvas
to paint the clouds,
it is your spine that declares itself:
arching,
your arms stemming out like tender shoots
to hang sheets in the sky.

IV   *Red Poppy*

Lost Sister

1

In China,
even the peasants
named their first daughters
Jade—
the stone that in the far fields
could moisten the dry season,
could make men move mountains
for the healing green of the inner hills
glistening like slices of winter melon.

And the daughters were grateful:
they never left home.
To move freely was a luxury
stolen from them at birth.
Instead, they gathered patience,
learning to walk in shoes
the size of teacups,
without breaking—
the arc of their movements
as dormant as the rooted willow,
as redundant as the farmyard hens.
But they traveled far
in surviving,
learning to stretch the family rice,
to quiet the demons,
the noisy stomachs.

2

There is a sister
across the ocean,
who relinquished her name,
diluting jade green
with the blue of the Pacific.
Rising with a tide of locusts,
she swarmed with others
to inundate another shore.
In America,
there are many roads
and women can stride along with men.

But in another wilderness,
the possibilities,
the loneliness,
can strangulate like jungle vines.
The meager provisions and sentiments
of once belonging—
fermented roots, Mah-Jongg tiles and firecrackers—
set but a flimsy household
in a forest of nightless cities.
A giant snake rattles above,
spewing black clouds into your kitchen.
Dough-faced landlords
slip in and out of your keyholes,
making claims you don't understand,
tapping into your communication systems
of laundry lines and restaurant chains.

You find you need China:
your one fragile identification,
a jade link
handcuffed to your wrist.

You remember your mother
who walked for centuries,
footless—
and like her,
you have left no footprints,
but only because
there is an ocean in between,
the unremitting space of your rebellion.

Spaces We Leave Empty

The jade slipped from my wrist
with the smoothness of water
leaving the mountains,

silk falling from a shoulder,
melon slices sliding across the tongue,
the fish returning.

The bracelet worn since my first birthday
cracked into thousand-year-old eggshells.
The sound could be heard
ringing across the water

where my mother woke in her sleep crying thief.
Her nightgown slapped in the wind
as he howled clutching his hoard.

The cultured pearls.
The bone flutes.
The peppermint disks of jade.

The clean hole
in the center, Heaven:
the spaces we left empty.

A Dream of Small Children

Toast crumbles in my mouth.
The walls of the house
curve like bare ribs
through which light traces,
opaque and milky. I skim
over these loose foundations
as if in a fish bowl—hemmed in,
haunted.

The sky is bandaged with white gauze.
A jet slits open the belly of clouds.
I mistake the trembling for thunder
and race out to snatch the laundry,
your clean, square handkerchiefs.
I wring them into diapers and knots.

Somewhere, I suppose, there are still
Eskimos who skin whales
quickly but gently,
submerging their ice blue hands
into warm sacs.
Eat the ripe ovaries like fruit,
wasting nothing,

while I mourn
and dream of small children;
what their noises
and hunger would be like
to this unleavened silence.

Having already decided on what must be done,
what we cannot have right now,
you turn back to your medical pages,
learning how to suture and save
the failing;
how to cut skillfully and neatly
the unwanted.

The Violin Teacher

for Patricia

She would wait
in the cool dust
of the plumeria trees
outside the violin teacher's house,
listening to the student
whose lessons came before her hour.
His playing made her nervous;
the notes scratched
like the scrawny music of chickens,
chasing the doves from their branches.
In the late afternoon heat,
she wore her batik dress,
the one woven with leaves.

Hurrying out of the house,
the young boy would avoid her
sitting there pale in the shade;
the white flowers
drifting silently around her like butterflies.

The bamboo slats were always drawn
to screen out the heat and the insects.
The violin teacher preferred the dark;
sunlight made him feel exposed.
When he played for his students,
he would insist that they close their eyes,
saying, "You can't see music."
Once she disobeyed and peeked
and was surprised, the soothing sounds
were spun from jerky, seizured movements.

She watched his body reel in spasms,
his face twitching, contorting into a demon's mask.
She never looked again.

They rarely spoke.
Upon arriving, he would nod to her
from the corner where he stood
preparing a medicinal drink,
the color and texture of ox blood.
The room reeked of eucalyptus and menthol,
like a forest she would often think.
He sometimes rubbed his hands in ointment.

When he was calm,
he would nod to her again.
Taking out her grandfather's violin,
she would slowly begin to play.
He sat facing the wall,
turning only to interrupt her rough passages.

In the quiet spaces,
he would place his bony fingers
over her moist hands,
guiding them along
the swan neck of the violin.
She ached until her fingers knew the places
where the music could be found
as if it were of her own body;
as he unlocked her callused fists,
loosening them
to feel out the music.
It was the only passion
he permitted himself.

Untouched Photograph of Passenger

His hair is brilliantined.
It is black and shiny
like patent leather.

He cannot be more than twenty:
his cheeks are full,
his face is smooth as a baby's,
though one pockmark
above his right temple
about the size of a rice kernel
is detectable.
His mouth appears to be
curved over something almond shaped.
Perhaps, he is sucking on a sweet plum.

His suit is puckered
at the seams.
The shoulders are too narrow,
fitting badly;
probably stitched
in a lamplit tailor shop
hovering in a back alley.
But the necktie adds
the texture of raw silk;
the added touch signifying

that this is meant to be
a serious picture;
the first important photograph
he has ever had taken.
This will document

his passage out
of the deteriorating village.
He will save it
to show his grandchildren.
As if already imagining them,

his eyes are luminous.
He is looking ahead,
beyond the photographer
in the dark room
crouched under the black velvet cloth,
beyond the noisy cluttered streets
pungent with garlic and smoked chestnuts.

Rinsing through his eyes
and dissolving all around him
is sunlight on water.

Chinatown

1

Chinatowns: they all look alike.
In the heart
of cities. Dead
center: fish eyes
blinking between
red-light & ghetto,
sleazy movie houses
& oily joints.

A network of yellow tumors,
throbbing insect wings.
Lanterns of moths
and other shady characters:
cricket bulbs & roach eggs
hatching in the night.

2

Grandmother is gambling.
Her teeth rattle: Mah-Jongg tiles.

She is the blood bank
we seek
for wobbly supports.

Building
on top of one another,
bamboo chopstick tenements
pile up like noodles.
Fungus mushrooming,

hoarding sunlight
from the neighbors
as if it were rice.

Lemon peels
off the walls so thin,
abalone skins.
Everyone can hear.

3

First question,
Can it be eaten?
If not, what good
is it, is anything?

Father's hair is gleaming
like black shoe polish.
Chopping pork & prawns,
his fingers emerge
unsliced, all ten intact.

Compact muscles taut,
the burning cigarette
dangling from his mouth,
is the fuse to the dynamite.

Combustible material.
Inflammable.
Igniting each other
when the old men talk
stories on street corners.
Words spark & flare out,

firecrackers popping on sidewalks.
Spitting insults, hurled garbage
exploding into rancid odors:
urine & water chestnuts.

4

Mother is swollen again.
Puffy & waterlogged.
Sour plums
fermenting in dank cellars.

She sends the children
up for air.
Sip it like tea.

5

The children are the dumplings
set afloat.
Little boats
bobbing up to surface
in the steamy cauldron.

The rice & the sunlight
have been saved for this:

Wrap the children
in wonton skins,
bright quilted bundles
sewn warm with five spices.

Jade, ginger root,

sesame seed, mother-of-pearl
& ivory.

Light incense to a strong wind.
Blow the children away,
one at a time.

For A. J.: On Finding She's
on Her Boat to China

Little by little a dancer destroys herself
until both her legs are broken.—Howard Schwartz

The final barre upon your back split;
a bridge you could not cross.
Too old or too tired for that kind of instruction.
The floor cracked from under you;
a misplaced mirror or a winter's pond
gone too slick.
Now you're on to something firmer,
standing at the bow of the ship,
over water, but it is something
instinct taught you to swim in.
A familiar choreography,
a ballet designed in your bones. On this crossing,
nearing the shore, like grains of rice
your father's seeds
are flung out to you.
Ancestors come and relatives;
everyone is a distant cousin.
They wind your raw feet in tiger balm,
entomb the satin shoes in jars.
Dismembered jasmin:
withered petals, rejected, pale and estranged.
Healing, you concentrate on another part,
  moving south to the center where the sun is
warmer.

Your first son shall do a dragon dance
when you have finally come home,
having planted two feet into the ground.
  Gravestones or roots,
   you will begin from there.

V   The White Trumpet Flower

Hotel Genève

There are these quiet resemblances.
Tonight, here in the city,
hard streets soften after rain.
The smell of plants is in the air.

It was always raining
in Mexico City,
the summer we went there
when I was fourteen.

I kept a pristine journal then
when anything white pleased me.
I would fold secrets into each page
as though I were wrapping
jade fish into origami.

But there were things
I had no words for:
the matrons in the morning
who brought clean starched sheets
stacked like envelopes or tortillas.
I made no distinctions:
for me, everything was edible.

The women were beautiful
and music floated out into the streets,
leaving on the hems of their skirts:
a flounce of fluted edges,
violet on challis.

The same blue tint
of the hydrangea in glass,
here on the table,
now as I write.

Along the Chapultepec,
the crisp lettucelike trees
were filled with the sound of water.
In the hotel restaurant,
we looked out into a walled garden
while waiters poured watermelon drinks
clinking into glass.
I ate chicken sandwiches
lined with red peppers,
watching all the while,
the white tablecloth
defined by a long-stemmed rose.

During the summer months,
it rained in the hours
between noon and four.
My father went on walks.
My mother bought amethyst.

I stayed behind,
trying to find the words to describe
the phenomena of the world
opening up before me
like an anemone.

Leaning against the window,
I sat looking through the iron
railing of the balcony
to the city and the rain.
They merged into one plane of vision
with my breath clouding the glass.

Those afternoons alone,
the light shuddered
translucent upon my skin
as I eased into the bath.
The vapor condensed onto the mirror
like the humid windows
of the flower shops we had passed,

like the kitchen window, now
blurred with rain.
Water everywhere
this end of summer.
I breathe in its smell,
of things green and ferny.
Tonight,
I am filled with the steam
my warm body gathered,
wrapping the petals of itself
in a white towel.

From the White Place

for Georgia O'Keeffe

1. Blue Bones: Ghost Ranch

So dry, there are no flowers
to paint,
but this pelvic mountain
thrusting toward light and heat,
insistent: I hack slabs of it at breakfast,
lie prostrate against it at night;
an arthritic who cannot sleep,
tormented by bones and joints—exposed,
and it is still there.

When she came out west,
her frail fields
collapsed into tumbleweed.
She thought the wind had hollowed out her eyes;
she could find no relief, no color.
She arranged a still life,
removing the last wall of her house
to confront the lunar mountain,
jagged like a fistful of chamisas.
Certain of a simple equation:
how the ocean hurls itself
without hurting its own energy.

I am learning from the Indians,
to burn juniper,
to coax fear away,
to enter a clearing.
When the thunderheads come in August,
pushing out the desert's mute odors,

the Indians perform
the procedure-of-the-body:
dip one's head in lilac,
urge a strong thirst.
Then with bones
dry like a shepherd's eyes
searching the horizon for water,
they introduce you to your body.

2. Memories, Gallery 291

He wanted to show her
the space between a man and a woman,
the oceans and plains in between:
she endured the inspections
of her bones and wrists.
The first touch surprised her;
his lens felt like a warm skull.

She sat waiting, unafraid,
trusting the shapes her body would make
as he plotted terrains and objects,
her face—
things not generally regarded as beautiful.

This is how it must be
to feel the pull of the moon
lengthening your blood,
when it is you the moon seeks
and no ground nor trees to guide you.

In the absence of color,
he assembled the dark curves,
seaming passages,
endless negatives,

like this terrible wind,
this wonderful emptiness . . .

3. From the White Place

Out on the pink mesa,
the soft sandstone glowed
like the belly of a salmon.
I began breathing for the first time today,
knowing the first breath would hurt.

A Pale Arrangement of Hands

It has been raining all night
and into the morning.
I sit, listening to the rain,
my hands on the kitchen table.
Their knuckles, yellow white
like the tendons of a drumstick,
the skin pulled taut to make a fist.
I remember my mother's hands,
how nervous they always seemed
except when they were busy cooking.
Her hands would assume a certain confidence
then, as she rubbed and patted butter
all over a turkey as though
she were soaping and scrubbing up a baby.

I wonder what she would prescribe
in weather like this. In Wahiawa,
it rained even when the sun was shining
through the mock orange trees.
"Liquid sunshine," she used to say
to the three of us peering from the jalousies
as if it happened only here,
in this part of the world.
The rain fell like a fence around our house,
in big drops slapping the mud
with the sound of slippers approaching,
housewives from the neighborhood
shaking their umbrellas at the kitchen door.

We sat in rapt attention
as Mother served her girl friends
instant coffee and caramel candy.
We knew the mothers by their children:
the mother of the boy who had ringworm;
the mother of the girl with the eleven cavities.
Ours was the youngest mother—slender,
with a bright red flower mouth,
being partial to Calypso Coral
sold at the Kress makeup counter.
I liked to watch her apply the lipstick:
first, she would stretch her lips
back into a wide square smile,
smear on the waxy color
and then with a soundless smack,
she would leave her mouthprint
on some white tissue.
I think she was pleased
the day she discovered something else
for us to do on those rainy afternoons:
showing us how to make artificial carnations
out of those discarded tissues
with a couple of hairpins.

Down the hall in the end room
she shared with our father,
she let us watch an hour of cartoons;
allowing herself time to fix
the tuna casserole or the Vienna sausages.
We were permitted to drift through the house,
within its safe circumference,
its comfortable geography.
If we became restless,
the sandbox in the covered patio
was the farthest distance we could travel,
stopping short of the rain.

We were three mild lunatics
she found herself with each day
in a chicken-coop house:
one child singing to herself,
a crinoline worn on her head like a shroud;
another bringing gifts of wildlife,
mongoose and centipedes;
and the youngest, a boy who sat
pugnaciously in front of the dryer,
watching his flannel blanket swirl clean,
refusing to go anywhere without it.

For my mother,
the afternoons brought
the longest part of the day.
I remember the frustrated look
when we refused to nap;
if only we would close our eyes,
be good, try to sleep.
I have no children but as I sit here
with my hands on my lap
and the rain falling outside the window,
I realize what power we wielded
when we were young.
Sleep meant pretending. Lying still
but alert, I listened from the next room
as my mother slipped out of her damp dress.
The cloth crumpling onto the bathroom floor
made a light, sad sound.

January

There is a child
growing between us.

Last night it snowed.
I lay in the bed
beside the window
while you walked to be quiet
among the disappearing trees.

Earlier in the evening,
you had attended
the birth of a boy.
You were the first to carry
in your gloved hands
the warm and glistening body.

You were remembering
that weight as you came
to stand in the white field.
How surprisingly
heavy and determined
new life is, pressing itself
like snow upon the existing structures:
the houses and the night
where the sleeping dwell, fitfully.
The light at each window
becoming dimmer like a pulse
beneath the thickening
walls of ice, blue and iridescent.

The Seamstress

I work best in a difficult light,
proud of these intelligent hands
like blind fingertips pressing upon
the fine, irresistible seams.

This is my world; my work:
to occupy a lean-to of a room
with a tin roof that slants
so on one side, an entire
wall without windows.

My spine bent over the Singer
has over the years conformed
into the silhouette of a coat hanger.
If I move about, it is with the slow
descent of the spider,
attached to an invisible thread,
I let myself down off the chair.

It is my hands that take
their miraculous flight, flying
from the cloth they guide toward
the continuous drone of the needle.
Hands moist and white like lilies.
The white gloved hands of the magician.

I turn bolts of cloth into wedding dresses
like chiffon cakes in the summer.
The frayed mothers arrive with their daughters.
I pin them in the afternoon fittings,

drape the veil about their soft faces
as if it were mosquito netting.

2

Moving among the orchids this morning,
I see the straw hat and slippered feet
of my ninety-two-year-old father.
I am the second of his four unmarried daughters.

He leaves a trail of water
behind him, dragging the hose
through the grass, around the hedges.
The heavy-whiskered jackfruit are ripening.
He will pick them with a muslin sack
wired to the end of a fishing pole.

His attachment to the world
is in the daily application of a skill.
It is the cultivating of orchids,
the most highly evolved species of flowers.
For me, it is the deft turning
of a sleeve, a pleat, or a collar.

He carries a spray of the smallest
variety past the screen door, each orchid
delicately and elaborately unfurled
like the ornate headpieces
my mother would make from threads
of black silk when as a girl
she was a dollmaker's apprentice in Japan.

With her we lived in a world of miniatures.
The world got swallowed up
into the smallest square of concentration.
My sisters and I became nearsighted,

squinting in the hot, still room,
relying on our agile fingers
to duplicate with scraps of silk
a shrunken world. Ornamented dolls
no more than twelve inches high
holding musical instruments.
Looking up to meet the room
swirling as if in a cloud of insects,
there were times when we fell
to the floor from exhaustion
and the sudden readjustment of vision;
our legs still tucked, as we were taught, beneath us.

3

The dolls are encased in glass boxes
displayed like shrines around the room.
The last one was made twenty years ago
just before my mother died.
Haruko, my third sister, keeps them dusted,
plucking at the occasional termites
that squeeze through the glass corners
to gorge their amber bodies on the brocaded silk.

My eyes sting today again
as though one of my sisters
nearby were peeling onions.
We each keep to our discreet part of the house,
crossing polite paths to murmur over meals.

It seems I have always lived
in this irregular room, rarely needing
to see beyond the straight seams that fit neatly,
the snaps that fasten securely in my mind.
The world for me is the piece of cloth

I have at the moment beneath my hands.
I am not surprised
by how little the world changes.
My father carrying the green hose
across the grass, a ribbon of water
trickling down his shoulder,
staining the left pocket
of his gray, loose-fitting shirt.
The wedding dresses each white, dusty summer.
Someone very quiet once lived here.

Glossary

Abiquiu (ăb′ĭ kū), small town in northern New Mexico.

chamisa (chă mē′ să), desert shrub.

Chapultepec (chă pŭl′tĕ pĕk), park in Mexico City.

Edo (ĕ′dō), present-day Tokyo.

Hoolehua (hō′o lĕ hŭ′ä), small town on the island of Molokai, Hawaii.

ikebana (ē kē′bä nä), Japanese art of floral arrangement.

kiawe (kĭ ä′vĕ), any of several mesquites introduced into Hawaii.

koi (coy), Japanese word for carp.

lilikoi (lĭ′lĭ koi), edible fruit belonging to the passion-flower.

shakuhachi (shä kōō′hä chĭ), five-holed Japanese bamboo wind instrument based on the pentatonic scale. The unusual mouthpiece allows the player to bend the sound into many subtle forms. The characteristic sound is melancholy. "Depicting the Cranes in Their Nest" and "Bell Ringing in the Empty Sky" are two names of classical pieces.

ti (tĭ), woody and leafy plant belonging to the lily family.

ukiyo-e (ū kē′yō ä), Japanese wood-block prints that flowered in the seventeenth century and declined in the nineteenth century, depicting scenes of everyday life, especially of and for the urban classes. They were called "pictures of the floating world" because of their pre-occupation with the pleasures of the moment.

Wahiawa (wä′hĭ ä wä), small town on the island of Oahu, Hawaii.

wahine (wä′hĭ nĕ), Hawaiian word for women.

Waialua (wä ĭ′ ä lŭ′ä), sugar mill town in northwest Oahu, Hawaii.

Acknowledgments

Acknowledgment is made to the following journals and anthologies for poems, or earlier versions of poems, published in them.

ASIAN-PACIFIC LITERATURE: *Chinatown, Lost Sister*
BAMBOO RIDGE: *Easter: Wahiawa, 1959; Hoolehua; Leaving; Tribe; Waialua; The White Porch; The Youngest Daughter*
DARK HORSE: *The Violin Teacher*
THE GREENFIELD REVIEW: *A Dream of Small Children, Chinatown, Picture Bride, Spaces We Leave Empty*
HAPA: *From the White Place, Stray Animals, The White Trumpet Flower*
HAWAII REVIEW: *Beauty and Sadness, Chinatown, For A. J.: On Finding She's on Her Boat to China, Ikebana*
NEW ENGLAND POETRY ENGAGEMENT BOOK: *Black Iris, Sunflower for Maggie*
RAMROD: *Untouched Photograph of Passenger*
SEAWEEDS AND CONSTRUCTIONS: *Seed*
TALK STORY: *An Orchid, Lost Sister*
TENDRIL: *Blue Lantern, Father and Daughter, For My Brother, Girl Powdering Her Neck, Hotel Genève, January*
WEST BRANCH: *Birthmarks, The Seamstress*

I wish to thank Mrs. George E. Brewer for her love and support, John Unterecker for his encouragement, and Kathleen Spivack for her invaluable teaching and friendship. I am also grateful to Stephen Dobyns for his suggestions.